T0161779

THERE ARE NO NAMES FOR RED

THERE ARE NO NAMES FOR RED

poems by

Chris Abani

paintings by

Percival Everett

RED HEN PRESS | LOS ANGELES, CALIFORNIA

There Are No Names for Red

ISBN: 978-1-59709-457-3
Library of Congress Catalog Card Number: 2009930299

Printed in China

The Annenberg Foundation, the James Irvine Foundation,
and the National Endowment for the Arts partially support Red Hen Press.

Published by by Red Hen Press
www.redhen.org
First Edition

DECICATION

{ CHRIS ABANI }

For Sarah

{ PERCIVAL EVERETT }

For Beth

ACKNOWLEDGEMENTS

{ CHRIS ABANI }

Some of these poems have appeared in
Blackbird, *Diode*, *Crate* and *World Literature Today*.

Many thanks to Percival Everett who let me in.

{ PERCIVAL EVERETT }

My Thanks to Chris for his friendship.

THERE ARE NO NAMES FOR RED

I

The way desire is a body eroding
into a pile of salt marked by a crown of birds:
and black. This fall is not rain, grain too subtle
for that dissolution. A constellation wrapped
in a stitch spreading like sand charting
thread across time, a tender weave
and hope. This is resurrection.

II

And the sky is red
                    And the moon
And light is this rain.

This is all the terror we can bear:

        the moment between flame
and where shadow begins
        but only so much as can be cupped
in a child's palm

and yet to say: the loved one
        has slipped to ghost.

III

What attempts survival here has no words
but hunger. A white backcloth that devours
the blackening. Then red cut in lines thick
as paste and obscuring the once figurative.
This desire wears cerements of yellow and sun.
And at the edge of this world, a box of wood
and canvas; light and light and light.

IV

Everything here can so easily turn to mud
and the recalcitrance of dead leaves and bugs.
There is hair here too. Not so much animal as rough.
I speak now of sorrow, of weight beyond measure.
There is a drowned woman in the dark swirl.
This paint, buoyant and light, eddies.

V

Whatever guilt drives this brush is nocturnal and heavy
with the smell of the cramped darkness under the stairs.
But night will not be blamed. What good are words
when the green light over the ocean is all we need?

VI

What passes for night here has more to do with the place
where the body is flayed open to sorrow and wonder.
The boy on the bridge drops a feather into a lost river.
A rusting lawn dreams of grass rude and fescue.
A match held down to tobacco still burns with an upward flame.
There is no truth here.
Dutifully the mist comes down the mountain.

VII

That lone shoe on the curb, foot turned to the wind, the road south.
Snow complicates the purity. Also sand;
Sand and grains that rub. Persistence and the silt.
The eternal shifting that erases all that is built.

VIII

Winter is defeated by a flock of geese flying towards the sun.
The sea is only as lonely as a single conch, or a sand dollar
fritted away on an impossible dream. Even this bold black line.
The Igbo believe the sun is only the aura of a creature we have
no name for. What is song here is ritual in another language.

IX

Even god must be astonished by it all.
Rain in the afternoon is always a surprise.
My first death was a butterfly.
The smell of Earl Grey mocks Proust.
But you're 39 now, she said. Do you still need
that hurt little boy? This line flowers up like a tree
in a red night but curves with the weight of lynching.
How can the moon be so blind?
Blake on Paxil? No tygers burning, that's for sure.
Non-committal lines that won't speak to each other and yet
the narrow gutter between them overflows
with the dirty water of all that is unsaid.
In rooms without names, Aga Shahid
Ali is still mourned with a circling grief.

22

X

When I returned from Auschwitz brimming with sorrow
and love I said, I will write a poem so profound it will
core the earth like an apple. Instead all I can say is:
daises have grown over the train tracks and a sparrow
lays blue eggs high in a tree like an incinerator chimney.
Percival's cat was called Cat.
Look closely at that painting. See the outline of her x-rays?
Jim was the Crow he carried on his left shoulder.
It grew strong and flew away but left a heavier weight.
This is no parable.

XI

That woman in a New York café cannot escape what it means
to sound like a Boer. If I were a better man, I would have compassion.
The thing is this: the dead, they won't stay buried. Emily said, about the woman
on the bus; she said are you going to the other side?
How easy it is for light reflecting off a polished wood floor to bend into metaphor.
Fire, water and mud. What a curious way to make a body.
Gravity wasn't the apple to Newton's head and yet he claims discovery.
But the moment you point to the black dog shivering against the red door
in the relentless rain, you lose it.

XII

Goldsworthy arranges daises, a meditation in the crook of the stream
with all the awe of the Neanderthal burying their dead.
The water takes the gift.
Is this how you get fish to make butter?
I remember every detail of everything my father inflicted on me
to erase his fear of loving me. I walk the stations of that pain
with all the relish of a self-flagellating
monk. I know something of pilgrimage.

XIII

Crocodiles in the river remind us every gift is hard won.

Perhaps it is the mud that makes the arrow-tips of rice so green.

The problem with caves is that we must enter them.

Ghosts in the morning rain. When it is over,

the rain is never enough.

I hated the Mau Mau growing up. They killed

women who looked like my mother.

They wore the face of my father. I have to

throw this baby out with the bathwater.

XIV

In the end it just happens.

Reasons are only logs to bank the fire of hope.

In Rwanda, before the genocide, the word for rape was the same as marriage.

The idea of gestural fragments.

These are the spells: ant's eggs for falling out of love.

The ghosts of washing drying on the line, like birds weaned at home.

The urge is to migrate, restless.

Some of our truest conversations are in diners.

My hands have known this experience,

the making and breaking of my spirit in this craft,

held. In the nebulous frame of words.

Those stormy symphonies of Beethoven—

figures of impossible dimensions.

XV

There is something soft here. Smooth as a stone in water.
A trick of the light perhaps, or this; the cold nonchalance
of fate and beauty is nothing more than this
canvas this skin and the hope we covet.

XVI

Also in other non-intended ways but touching. Canvas
heavy with salt after salt and salt and water,
the brine a knowledge and this sail unannealed like skin
and my grandmother dying, dying in the shower and water
all around her. This is not intended and yet the distance between
almost perfect and complete chaos is a hair's breath.
Loose strands unravel and follow an idea.
In Berlin there are brass caps, square and green with time,
set into the paving stones that trip you.
You look down and see the names of those taken to the camps.
Stubbing stones they call them. Stolpersteine. And nobody knows
exactly who put them there. Turkish women in black
descend on us like a gaggle of crows. Yes, I said gaggle.
And what is gained? And what is lost?
What begs silence here is beyond even that.

XVII

There is no doubt, kin is my search. I want to connect these lines
to the ones charting my face in the faded mirror of time. This need is visceral.
And yet ideas are robust as plump well-fed geese and this is the lie of it.
I don't seek kin here. I seek adoration. I seek worship. I seek the voice of my father.
First of all, I do not buy into mythological figures, so fuck Odin and his tree,
yet wounded trees mark the spot, an itch unreachable. But still gazing Odin summons
the runes. I say futhark you say tomatoes. And the deep is this dark mark across the soul.
This poem is an animal Terence says and sips some coffee. That way language can
sprint across the desert filling it with an oasis. And why not?
This pure flame, this pure fire, and these scars our nomadic natures carve across us.
If this poem is an animal it's all Percival's fault. If this poem is an animal.

XVIII

Under a relentless sun in a small Mexican town,
three old women in black
 gather before the startled white of the church.
A little girl watches from across the street.
If a newspaper falls from the hand of an old man dying
in a chair, fanning into a tarot spread on the floor and
no one is there to see it, does it make a sound?

XIX

My grandfather once said the Milky Way is God's clock.

XX

A taxi through night and palms that gather desire like dew.
A window opens onto the hiss of rain on tarmac and this smell
is old earth, and a grave, grace even and flowers rotting
at the edge of time, at the edge of the road where a child died.
It's like the way the little white plane hovers on the vastness of
the ocean between Godthab and St. John's. The Atlantic tamed
momentarily by the flight information screen and yet in the dark cabin,
all that keeps it aloft is the soft breathing of the other sleeping passengers.
And nothing is lonelier in the world at this moment
than that little white cross on the expanse of blue screen.
Faith is something like this, I imagine. Not of God. But of a pen or a brush
held up like the last flaming torch of the century, and yet flimsy—
this desire of the artist to keep the blue from swallowing it all up.
Like something that happens only at night.
Like a lie and desperation so thick you can breath it. Moments
like this, the skin widens to the lover's touch and the back arches to whispers.
Even this cannot keep the void away. The mid-Atlantic ridge is a
mountain under the sea, and its active volcanoes widen the ocean bed.
I want to say, "This one's on me, Mr. Freud! Can I get an Amen?"
Still we're lost in that vast blue and I think how did the Vikings ever find
anything down there? Stumbling about in the dark like still unrealized id's.
There is nothing clear about it, nothing lasting about this clarity.
I will do it different, I say. I will. As if the threat of death is not a smell
I will lose in a few days. This terror comes in without knocking.
Like a familiar lover intruding into the bathroom as I pee.
I will lose even this when it mingles with the old smell of her wetness
and I will forget and drown us both in wine and regret.

XXI

This thing is a too exclusive love for color,
a burden on the canvas. Something Jesus would get
but only as Muddy Waters screaming in a riot of shadows.

XXII

There is a blur of black on green like the unruly shadow of some night be-
fallen building, a shawl wrapped around a hooker's too tight too short skirt.
Or the contrite line of an old nun bent black from shame and
the pleasure of beads rubbed between sensuous fingers and the prayers
savored like divine sweatmeats. Or perhaps it is just me, or the dark
glimpse I catch from the corner of my fearful eye. Or death.
Ah, but the green, fescue grass and the dark of loam.

XXV

In Mexico City's metro, my friend tells me, is a stop called Ethiopia.
Just that. And a lion's profile stamped into the concrete walls.
There are catacombs honeycombing the world.

XXVI

Someone please tell Carlos Drummond de Andrade that there is a stone
in the middle of the road. I saw it too; finally.
Carlos has been looking for that stone since my grandmother
borrowed it to sharpen her knife. It was the onions, you see.
My knife wasn't so sharp either the day I cut the throat on my childhood.
It's not hard to kill a childhood.
Did you never see your father slap your mother?
Did you never feel the shame?
Never thought, yes, shut up, mum?
Did her eyes never forgive you?
Cats are easier to forgive. Even when their rabid bite
costs you twenty-six injections to the stomach.
Riding her bike in the slight drizzle each knee catching in my throat
the young woman and white. The flash of underwear and I am six again.

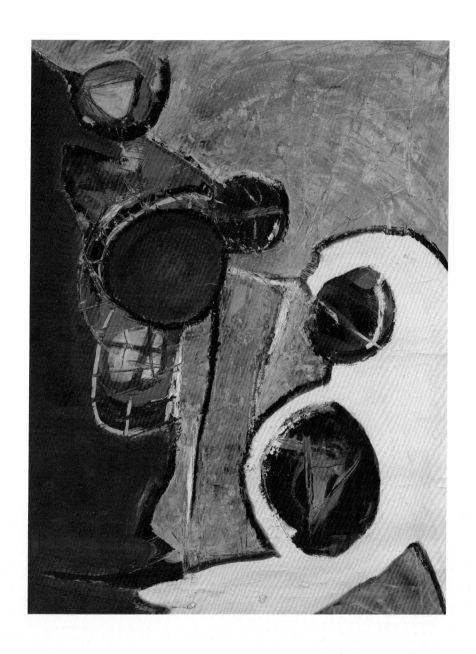

XXVII

How nicely they've fixed the bullet holes in the walls,
in Rwanda. Painted bright petals around some areolas.

XXVIII

A painting is never the thing it says it is.
Of course this is poetry, every human breath is sublime.
Ask Paolo. In cold caves, with the instance of a flash he captures
only a breath. And then another. Clouds of blue and hope.
This is a sculpture, he says. Even this. I believe him. Percival doesn't
paint the sea. Yet all of his canvases are full of water. Maybe
I shouldn't have gotten back on the bicycle after that bad fall that crushed
my balls. You're ten, Mark said. If you don't you never will. Just do it.
Was that a Nike ad even then?

XXIX

Percival says it's not for the fishing. It's for the river. The sudden bend
that holds all the light in a man's soul. There is something like awe in his eyes.
He looks down and takes a bite of Salmon. The fish is good. Pete's is open late.
We both like that. Nocturnes.

Sometimes a goat lifts a bottle. But we always stop short of the lips.
Alcohol goes better with Pieces. We have none of their grace.

XXX

In the end, there are no names for red but fire,
hydrant, apple, ball, heart, blood, sacrifice, and altar.
Look, my nephew says, fire engine.

CHRIS ABANI

Chris Abani's prose includes *Song For Night* (Akashic, 2007), *The Virgin of Flames* (Penguin, 2007), *Becoming Abigail* (Akashic, 2006), *GraceLand* (FSG, 2004), and *Masters of the Board* (Delta, 1985). His poetry collections are *Hands Washing Water* (Copper Canyon, 2006), *Dog Woman* (Red Hen, 2004), *Daphne's Lot* (Red Hen, 2003), and *Kalakuta Republic* (Saqi, 2001). He is a Professor at the University of California, Riverside and the recipient of the PEN USA Freedom-to-Write Award, the Prince Claus Award, a Lannan Literary Fellowship, a California Book Award, a Hurston/Wright Legacy Award, a PEN Beyond the Margins Award, the PEN Hemingway Book Prize & a Guggenheim Award.

Percival Everett

Percival Everett is the author of sixteen novels, three collections of short fiction, and two volumes of poetry. Among his novels are *The Water Cure* (2008), *Wounded, Glyph, Erasure, American Desert, For Her Dark Skin, Zulus, Cutting Lisa, Watershed,* and *God's Country.*

He is the recipient of the PEN Center USA Award for Fiction, the Academy Award from an American Academy of Arts and Letters, the Hurston/Wright Legacy Award, the PEN/Oakland-Josephine Miles Award for Excellence in Literature, and a New American Writing Award. His stories have been included in the Pushcart Prize Anthology and Best American Short Stories. He has served as a judge for, among others, the 1997 National Book Award for fiction and the PEN/Faulkner Award for Fiction in 1991. He teaches fiction writing and critical theory and is currently Distinguished Professor of English at the University of Southern California.